ALLEN GINS[BERG, WHY ARE YOU] LONELY? / FRIEDRICH NIETZSCHE, WHERE HAVE YOU GONE?

I TRY TO MEAN IT WHEN I SMILE

THE N WORD

I ONCE KNEW A TIGER

VISIONS OF MY SAVIOR

BY MARINO

PRINTED BY DERUSHA PUBLISHING LLC

Books printed by Derusha Publishing LLC may be purchased for educational, business, or sales promotional use. For more information, please write:
Special Markets Department
Derusha Publishing LLC
6-05 Saddle River Rd #103
Fair Lawn, NJ   07410
USA

Snow falls slow and light

Quickly covering up names

In hearts on the ground.

A Note from the Author

I'm told that fifty-five-hundred word poems are somewhat unusual, and so require some sort of explanation. I am generally of the opinion that art, when explained by the artist, ceases to be art, but becomes decoration, so, perhaps a short history will suffice.

When I started putting words next to each other in the back of a class about the personality of Abraham, I did not think for an instant that it would end up covering fourteen pages of printed paper, and completely decimating my notebook. I started writing, inspired by Nietzsche's demand that I become who I am. I wanted to write a piece that defined who I am by chronicling the way I see the world around me. I wanted to write a manuscript that I could die clutching, but had no idea how. I decided to start, and so with the backdrop of Torah words behind me, I wrote obscenities. I had planned to start, but obviously not to stop; somewhere around ten pages I showed it to a friend, wondering if I was going to be stuck writing it for the rest of my life.

That's when he mentioned Howl.

"The beginning is just like Howl," he said.

"Howl?"

"Howl for Carl Solomon." I must have heard of it. "It's a famous Ginsberg poem."

"Oh yeah, I think I read that one time. It's pretty long, too. Right?"

He insisted I go home and read the whole thing. That night, i was reborn. I was already familiar with Ginsberg; "A Supermarket in California" was and still is one of my favorite poems. But when I read "Howl" I was transformed. The form, it's true, is eerily similar. The poems are completely different, Ginsberg being more of a hipster than I. But every word he wrote, and every fallen genius he mentioned I fell in love with. I needed to know more about Ginsberg, about Carl Solomon, about Jack, and Neal, and Burroughs and anyone who could write.

I tried to understand every meaning to the word "Beat" (and there are many).

It is taught that a dream is one sixtieth prophecy, and so I tried to dream. This is my dream, this is my reality. This is my America, as I see it from the smoking banks of Lethe.

Allen Ginsberg, I am lonely. Friedrich Nietzsche, I am lost.

America, I was a dreamer when I was a child. I'm not sorry.

The Prisoner at the Gates of Dawn

Allen Ginsberg, Are You Lonely?

Where Have You Gone, Friedrich Nietzsche?

I've seen the legends of generations turn to dust while being pissed

on by hoodie wearing hipsters toting bags of heroin disguised

as porn magazines and vibrators.

I've seen wisdom tossed aside to make way for gun-toting fascists

screaming of ecstasy and sweet release.

For children, who, smoking apathetic mushrooms in atheistic

convents, watched reality fade to cell phones and beepers.

Who stuck Doobies up their asses for inspiration, then wondered if

the ensuing orgasm was from the pot, or the cock up the

anus.

Who ran from Atlanta to New York, all the while aiming for Denver,

or Palestine.

Who dreamed of homicides, and suicides, and patricides, and

theocides galore.

Who slept with red-necked chickens laying eggs of solid gold.

Who sucked cough drops and ice cubes through straws of colored glass.

Who sang of hookers and silver chains while leaving out the 'R's with Bostonian grace.

Who lay beneath the stars in air-conditioned tents, all the while whining of missed episodes and unnatural heat.

Who craved jelly donuts and candy canes which were later regurgitated in the sink.

Who played guitar at best friend's parties, strumming the infamous G–C–D.

Who sat in corners writing poetry, while all around them life went on.

Who sun-bathed on beaches full of seagulls with blackberries full of sand and hundred-dollar sweatshirts.

Who sat uninspired in lecture halls waiting for someone, or something to somehow show them the way.

Who bought essays off the Internet, and later called a street-bum lazy.

Who flipped burgers for national amusement while giving blow-jobs
    on cable T.V.

Whose parents paid for their porn career, while angel headed losers
    watched someone better in unlit basements.

Who contracted aids from dirty needles while snorting million-
    dollar coke with eighty-year-old bankers.

Who played "punk rock" in stadiums, singing of heartbreak while
    fucking pop stars and signing record deals.

Who inspired murderers, and thieves, then spoke of the poverty
    cycle and crime.

Who rallied for civil rights and freedom, only to slander the god of
    another.

Who chanted wildly for a pay raise, then quit anyway to collect food
    stamps and unemployment.

Who, upon hearing the bells ring in the far off distance, dropped to
    their knees and praised Jehovah, Mohamed, and Sponge Bob.

Who, in times of desperation, turned to rapists to show them the way
    to salvation.

Who spat in the faces of their elders, while looting rotten corpses for

   a simple fix.

Who died of cancer three times over, but came back to see the

   second coming fail.

Who traveled to Venice, and stayed there in Venice, only to drown in

   their sleep.

Who lost their virginity in back-seats stained with cum and saliva

   from a man who never called them back.

Who killed hamster upon hamster in cold-blooded vigor, staring

   intently at the carnage with both hands down their pants.

Who bashed gays, blacks, Koreans, and Jews everyday, and upon

   returning home burned old family photos.

Who set nights ablaze with kerosene and paperbacks, flames flying

   through the evening sky.

Who dropped atom bombs and tear gas on their next-door

   neighbors with the wind blowing into their faces.

Who maxed out their credit card buying name-branded murder

   from china town and Beijing.

Who refused to conform, by wearing black and ripping jeans,

    throwing cash money at the newest style to hit the scene.

Who "fought" to keep their country safe from home sweet home

    while far away men fell and died to pay for the oil to cook

    their meats, move their cars, and lubricate their asses.

Who moved lines on a map back and forth, crying "forward to

    salvation!" from the comfort of pressurized cabins.

Who made brave sacrifices and decisions by sending their men off to

    the desert to secure another opium-filled field for the

    emperor.

Who worshiped the morals they were taught as a child all the while

    ignoring rules five through ten.

Who followed blindly while the front line marched silently off the

    cliff.

Who flung themselves at bullets flying through the air with backspin

    and hatred, chopping violently through bodies in search of

    plutonium to call its home.

Who sat on merry-go-rounds tossing grenades, watching with glee

    as women and children ran for their lives.

Who died for their countries, and were left to rot on the battlefield,

    proud of their sacrifice.

Who choked on their own elbows, ravenously consuming themselves

    in a fervor of hate.

Who robbed their own children, looting the mansions on Christmas

    Eve while over for Chinese food dinner.

Who worshiped false prophets, and when the time came crucified

    themselves to make way for their successors to die in vain.

Who hid in the bushes, and sat in the treetops looking through the

    bedroom windows of movie stars and teenagers.

Who spoke out of ignorance then killed millions in jungles and

    forests to cover up their lies.

Who screamed of agony and pain at a ripped sweater, dirtied jeans

    or lost plaything while children half a world away slaved

    over fabrics and sewing machines.

Who moved down to Florida in the evening of their lifetimes, hiding

   in the sand from grim defeat.

Who traveled to Los Angeles, Chicago and New York looking for a

   solution to their farm boy blues.

Who traveled from Kansas to Arkansas speaking slowly of Ohio,

   waiting for the Tin soldiers and plasma guns.

Who waited in vain for the age of reason and died lonely and cold,

   never having the courage to stand up to the fury of

   hailstorms and fire which spewed from the southerly winds

   of reform.

Who sucked endless cock and balls, adding in a complement here, a

   falsehood there, all the while keeping both eyes fixed on the

   road ahead and the gold beneath the sand covered beaches.

Who doubted the prophets, slandered the poets, and crucified the

   saviors, all in the name of religion and god.

Who quoted the scriptures and prayed in the temples, dropping to
their knees in bouts of prayer; and later that night remained
on their knees with the red lights shining and the cash
flowing in.

Who spoke of reform and family values while Vegas paid for ballots,
commercials, and toilets made of gold.

Who leaned forward in their seats to better hear the lies of ages past
and futures not with coming.

Who barred windows, locked doors, and bullet-proofed skylights to
keep out the mosquitoes, meanwhile caging the songbirds
and tigers.

Who stared at the sun, then the moon, then the stars while digging
deeper to the core of the earth.

Who journeyed to Canterbury, to Bethlehem, and to Mecca in search
of florescent light bulbs to last for eternity.

Who wrote love letters in leetspeak, abbreviations and Swahili,
leaving their sweethearts in suspense to the meaning behind
the letters L-U-V.

Who drank power drinks and flavored water, ingesting more poison

and daggers than Caesar himself.

Who got a job in New York, bought a cat, and never again ventured

outside their central park apartments.

Who sat stoned in basements, attics, and fading living rooms

wondering where they took a wrong turn on their journey to

Jerusalem.

Who jumped from illuminated rooftops and towers, landing

gracefully on the ground before cowering in fear at how big

the ants beneath their feat had become.

Who wrote to historians and poets alike, commenting on the

inconveniences of the past, and asking if it could please be

changed.

Who saw nothing, knew nothing, and cared nothing for the billions

who died beneath their feat, the cries of freedom emanating

from their ever-parched throats as they faded to the dark

knight's serenity.

Who smoked cannabis in dollar bills, burning the franklins and hash

        leaves alike.

Who babysat for bags of heroin and plutonium, sitting obediently in

        front of T.V. screens and microwaves waiting for the beep.

Who cowered in their sleep, putting up barricades of slime and rot

        hoping with all their might that that it would stop the rain.

Who took gold watches, gold fillings, and golden eyeballs off the

        dirty corpses of the fallen, stripping the body of all its

        treasures before sending it downriver to burn in the coal

        plants.

Who drove tanks, flew bombers, and threw hand grenades at second

        cousins, adopted parents, and best friend's sisters.

Who hunted for meat, for fur, for fats, and for sport.

Who blessed the queen, hailed the crown and threw their freedoms

        at her feet screaming "take them, take them, take them all to

        glorify your name".

Who went deaf and blind to the calls of the falconers, acting out of

    ignorance, missing their cues and committing atrocities all in

    a string of misunderstandings.

Who praised their leaders, quoting party doctrine and patriotic

    mottoes.

Who beat on five year olds, and egged old houses trying desperately

    to gain the approval which never came.

Who listened to orchestras, played pianos, and wrote great literature;

    feigning culture as they murdered millions in the streets.

Who hid in the basements when the rapture came, fearing

    purgatorial pain as the hurricane passed and the waters died

    down.

Who were dragged through silent waters, darkened valleys and dog

    filled barnyards.

Who read playboy mags for the articles, exercising hands behind

    closed doors.

Who salivated at polo shirts and collars raised, ignoring completely

    the bodies to which they clung.

Who quoted poetry, cited great authors, and read from lyric books,
speaking others minds at every turn, yet failing to have their
own.

Who raced in stock car derbies, wasting gasoline paid for in the
blood of their sons and daughters in deserts across the sea.

Who sold tomaco products, ex-filled barley and opium rice.

Who laughed heartily at cartoon mice, then wore black and asked
questions like "Why did they do it?" and "Where is my son?".

Who drank up the ruffies, gulping down spiked drinks with
unintended velocity and force.

Who bought spare livers from the starving poor, breaking in their
third or fourth with alcohol and poppy drinks.

Who ejaculated on prisoners of war, laughing loudly and speaking
without words.

Who videotaped the new recruits crawling through the mud after
being repeatedly raped and tortured with dull blades and
broken light bulbs.

Who watched their best friends die on network news, not shedding a

tear before flipping to their favorite soap opera channel.

Who listened to the lottery, tuned in to the newscast, and ignored

their parents' cries for help.

Who needed a weather man to know which way the wind blew.

Who suffocated in pillowcases, drowned in swimming pools, and

found a million other ways to die young and useless.

Who went bowling in dark alleys and side streets, completely

ignorant of the friends who got left behind until it was their

turn to be snatched into the darkness.

Who spiraled lower, lower, lower; lower until they hit rock bottom

and beat on the cold stone floor begging to be admit into the

under-chambers of the hell they'd been chasing all their

lives.

Who sucked the life out of vampire bats, frankensteins, and

werewolves howling in the night at the concrete moon.

Who saw in their lifetimes the overarching reach of all fears and

evils as they sat silently in the back-seats of SUVs, ATVs,

monster trucks and dirt bikes.

I've seen strippers yelling loudly in tone-deaf voices while beat

boxers lost their rhythm.

* * *

I was there in Paris, when movie stars and cyber nerds hit the scene

with camera crews and STDs.

I was there in Denver, when beats were killed, words were fried, and

running through the streets were blood-crazed feminists

with tits of iron and led.

I was there in Alabama, when crosses burned, people died, and little

children worked their hands to the bone.

I was there in England, when misled rejects, newly released from

institutions to make way for American politicians took to the

streets and plazas calling for Mary or Margaret.

15

When rivers overflowed, cities went under, and the cries for help

went unheard above the surface.

When synth beats took over, so persuasive in their simplistic rhythms

that submission was compulsive and obedience complete.

When two minutes hate rang from the speakers, and T.V. screens

shown with images of violence and death.

* * *

I was there in Dublin, when battle raged and brothers fell, cheering

loudly for the freedom they never won.

I was there in Cuba, in Russia, in America and in France, when

revolutions fell and dictators yelled, shooting the heroes of

Paris and of Nice.

I was there in Vatican City, when the rapture came and Jesus was

nowhere to be found.

I was there in Texas, when the oil wells ran dry, and

environmentalists were mined for their oily pimples and

pores.

When presidents were born, and the man from the future had not

the courage to slay the child he came back for.

When guns were fired, bullets flew, and sombreros fell five feet short

of the border.

When bleeding-hearts disease became a capital offense and slaying

instead of saving became the way of the land.

* * *

I was there in Africa, when children died, warlords grew rich, and

the cries of the people went dumb and unheard.

I was there in Springfield, when drunks lay forgotten, justice was

rotten, and old lady judges laid down justice that was neither

fair nor just.

I was there in Camden, when racists ruled town, bike gangs stopped

cars, and drug lords were considered merciful and fair while

down the block white folk sat in homes and dining cars

eating caviar and baby bones.

I was there in Nashville, when the blues rang true; the broken

fingers plucking strings after being beaten for dropping a

rock.

When dry cleaning stores were busy with work, steaming and

starching the white robes and hoods.

When sons hit their fathers, slept with their mothers, and appeared

on talk shows that aired all over the country.

When sisters were mothers, brothers were nephews, and everyone

was related through marriage or through sex.

* * *

I've seen visions upon visions left unseen, unhad, and unwanted.

I've seen lovers and haters joining hands in communal orgies in
 praise of the gods of Hollywood and crack.

I've seen cathedrals burn down, stained glass falling through the
 night with silent disdain.

I've seen silent walls of hidden plastic bend and melt with the
 petrified agony of minor chords and organ rhythms.

I've seen stone temples, metal altars, and silken garments all
 consumed by the flames with atomic might.

I've seen the faithful observers starve to death in lands of
 opportunity while far off across the oceans civilized men
 were singing songs and drowning babies.

I've seen cultured peoples take the streets with xenophobic fury;
 shattering glass, looting homes, and burning shops.

I've seen intelligent men with IQ's of infinity marching obediently
 with the pack: one foot forward to praise the leader.

I've seen godly men full of morals sit idly in their homes while the
 paper boy brings news of murder most foul in the back of
 death bringing vans and coughing pits.

I've seen geniuses driven to madness, running through the rivers of

    apple juice and milk, half-naked from the top down with

    carrots sticking out their asses.

I've seen hot-blooded losers in drag attire and cosplay dress, hoping

    to be picked as the next tragic hero.

I've seen brain-dead telepaths covered in chocolate and caramel,

    melting silently in the Siamese sun of New England.

I've seen retarded babies with AIDS outsmart game-show contestants

    with apparent ease as onlookers sat fat and lazy on the living

    room couch.

I've seen plutonium textbooks glowing with anticipation and thrill,

    ready to be cracked open for the first time in twenty years.

I've seen elderly gun nuts, climbing the Berlin wall screaming

    "Freedom Forever" before dying a million deaths and coming

    back to kill their heroes.

I've seen half-dressed romantics, half-dead elitists, and long

    forgotten hippies strolling through the war zones in predawn

    contemplation.

I've seen summer showers, winter flowers, and springs and falls that

ceased to be.

I've seen christs, fresh off the assembly line glowing with blood and

semen.

I've seen super psychic canines, sniffing drugs, lies, and intelligence.

I've seen suicidal dolphins, bleeding yellow-blue blood in the hours

before nighttime.

I've seen lovers kiss, silently embracing as the tick tock rang and the

days wore thin.

I've seen parents burying children with a heavy heart as war goes on

and the sands of time dissolve with their blood.

I've seen vinegar-covered hobos lie bleeding in the sun, skin burning

and itching like chicken pox from Krypton.

I've seen shit-covered babies eating grass, mud, and hermit crabs;

sobbing slowly, sleeping silently, and screaming with

agonizing stupidity: striking silver daggers through the hearts

of all within earshot.

I've seen galaxies destroyed, revolutions burn, and tyrants arise from

the ashes of their people's despair.

I've seen the shining light, the shrieking fury, and the creeping

inertia of bitter defeat on a one-way train to Hades and back.

I've seen misguided morons, Mormons, and mothers taking turns on

the night-watch over baby Jesus' cradle.

I've seen Cinderella, Hamlet, and Edmond Dantès locked saber to

saber in a fight to the death over Romeo and Juliet's lovechild

of thirteen.

I've seen Dylans, Rogers, and Walts die pen in hand, ink in their eyes,

and a feather through their hearts.

I've seen madmen die alone, rotting in the graveyards where they

met their first victims.

I've seen gods slain by men, their heads decapitated and stuck on a

pike hanging from the tree of knowledge.

I've seen madmen, Murderers, thieves and politicians; rapists and

pedophiles running for office, speaking of infinite vagina.

I've seen criminals beating inmates while the real thieves and

murderers sat in oval offices and Wall Street boardrooms.

* * *

I've seen word slingers with humble roots who sprouted to great

heights and died jumping off the tallest branch.

Who mourned their mothers before they died, bleeping out the cuss

words while she rotted alone in Pilgrim's State.

Who sat motionless and alone, writing silent movies and

lamentations at four-years-old.

Who lay lonely and cold waiting for a man, a woman, or a puppy to

lie beneath their thigh.

* * *

I've seen rodeo clowns who shot acid-water from flowers and

laughed like crazies on crack.

Who wielded axes and hoses, spewing blood and oil at children and

    tigers.

Who played harpsichord and xylophone like a newsman played

    flute.

Who took madness and ravings to a logical extreme, arguing with

    passion over obscene cases, absurd rulings, and extinct

    questions.

* * *

I've seen lonely old grubbers who strolled through the alleys and

    aisles asking for angels and avocados, and getting heartbreak.

Who pulled up in motorboats to the shores of Hades, watching the

    river of time and paradox.

Who whispered good riddance to the wind in the willows,

    meditating in the watermelons and the shadows.

Who fell from the cradle and drowned in the sea next to Ichorus,

    calling for the captain, the crewmen, or the prisoners of war.

I've seen moose wearing hipsters in pink and orange blood, bathing

     in the glory of nitwit fulfillment.

I've seen meteors fall from the sky, crashing slowly with divine fury

     as the men inside were crushed, and the rapists called it an

     act of god.

I've seen cities drown, countries starve, whole worlds turn to ash as I

     sat on death row on charges of sacrilege and prophecy.

I've seen devils, angels, bishops and pigs all spooning each other in

     rhythmic unison as the starry night fell and the ignorant

     soldiers marched through fields of barley and haze.

I've seen grown men huddled in corners, burning ancient art lest big

     brother find it in their homes.

I've seen lonely old misers carved of obsidian far outlasting the evil

     deeds which they wrought in their lifetimes.

I've seen vampires, dragons, warlords and magicians warring for

the fate of the galaxy as the last mortal man in all of England

succumbed to terror and awe.

I've seen fat filled postal men, delivering in rain, snow, and atomic

fallout.

I've seen outcasts throw potatoes, tossing wildly all the way to the

institutions, and still throwing eggs at the stars in their head.

I've seen poets pick poppies; pissing, prowling, and preaching prose

based bullshit and French filled feces, fingering pencils and

inkwells with noses, with ears, and with mouths.

I've seen jazz musicians, Blues Beloveds, and Rock and Roll super-

groups band together to fight the war against time and

money.

I've seen Indians cry and bleed, saying "when in Rome" while

building roads, extending the path from the first great trail to

the last great stand. Biding time 'til the final day, and the

finest love.

I've seen bedpans crack, spilling all of the menstrual blood which the

   angels mourned as young men died and killers fried in chairs

   of murder and justice.

I've seen life-bringing tubes squeezed shut and dry as the funding

   was pulled and the cash flow stopped along with the blood.

I've seen Vagabonds journey from Camden to alpine, telling tales,

   spreading lies, and jumping from pole to pole like Kerouac to

   Paterson.

I've seen dandelion chains inject poisonous peace and tranquility to a

   madness which was once genius and daisy.

I've seen rabbits die in tunnels and holes, digging endlessly and

   forgetting the sun as they drowned on the biggest wave in the

   sea.

I've seen self-professed madmen claim ecstasy and love, telling Uncle

   Jack of their travels to the beanstalk.

I've seen mummies rise and fall, growing like empires in the

   grasslands by the river and the locusts.

I've seen concrete shaped wristbands pointing to the cosmos as their

tails lit on fire with Molotov cocktails and glass blown

destruction.

I've seen men eaten alive, worms crawling and chewing as the wall

stood tall and the child screamed "Fall!".

I've seen ghetto-raised killers bathe in hot tubs and saunas while a

hundred miles away subterranean basements oozed with

homesick aliens huddled together for warmth.

I've seen penis-shaped simpletons plagiarize poorly, pulling an

adjective here, a proper noun there, altogether composing

something incoherent, inconceivable, and unoriginal.

I've seen political bimboes shrug off their failure, glazing over

potholes with frosting and dollar bills.

I've seen world renowned celebrities make it big by playing

computer games and watching blue ray disks, slowly

developing diabetes as the baby fat hardened and the

footballs lay forgotten in well-kept yards and developing

fields.

I've seen cell phones, beepers, and digital cameras ganging up on

tourists after melting together to form a condom shaped

behemoth made of plastic and lithium.

I've seen third-partied aristocrats shouting of false reforms while

countries burned and rockets left their marks.

I've seen rich men with homes in third world countries, take a stroll

through dick's backyard before returning to playboy

mansions.

I've seen golden combs and golden locks binding and clawing at the

slave driver's breath.

I've seen titans of three feet tall shooting thunder from their hands

and lightning from their ears.

I've seen fascist maids teaching hate of self, of love, and of orgy-less

prayer rooms.

I've seen balls of fire, of laughter, of teardrops, and of air.

I've seen devil laced losers in cancerous attire and redneck poetry

stare intently as the heavens blazed with the light of twelve

million eyes.

I've seen musicians of a brilliant nature who loved and lost without

regret until the day they were thrown off the penthouse roof,

suicide note in hand as they caused their own destruction.

Who locked hands with angels and demons, striking deals with god

to sell their souls.

Who left books in taxis for the public to see, and sobbed of remorse

when the car hit a truck, and the truck lit on fire.

Who wandered drunkenly through the streets of Tel Aviv, catching a

flight to south-west new jersey, and lost themselves with the

eggplant.

* * *

I've seen fields full of daises containing brainwashed children who

ran from their parents and drank up the kool aid.

Who praised the leader, with lima beans and joy.

Who sold out for UFOs, flying through the air as the hunch man

peddled wildly and the laymen bowed down.

Who sang songs of fishing, of heroes, and sluts.

* * *

I've seen socialist pigs that screamed in accents and squealed with

excitement and lies.

Who used the machines to cut up a horse, telling the others he was

sent to a spa.

Who wrote down the rules again and again, each time changing the

barnyard ideal.

Who drank with the men, and slept in their beds, playing the part of

the one who had left.

* * *

I've seen pirates chop bananas, dreaming fantasies while bombs

dropped before their sounds.

I've seen lion headed men with wings of eagles sink in the quick

      sand of ego-bred legends.

I've seen evil twins and horoscopes collide.

I've seen celluloid jump to life under the neon spotlight of

      supernatural prose.

I've seen cherry-flavored Alzheimer's patients whine on and on like

      a broken record while the ears of the youth stay clogged with

      headphones and paranoia.

I've seen anti-feminist abolitionists beat workers for arriving five

      minutes late.

I've seen stars explode, leaving ash and dust to rise and fall with

      mutant wolves.

I've seen civil wars fought in bunkers, the aeroplanes falling from

      the skies of Frankfurt and Leningrad.

I've seen species go extinct eating Aramaic turkeys and metaphors.

I've seen super saturated sand pits reject fool's gold and inhale glue-

      scented aerosol cans made of cubic zirconium and piss.

I've seen lies made of Kashmir lob plasma balls at lava lamps with
nostalgic pride.

I've seen paper fed vampire bats with bloodshot eyes and lightning
wings.

I've seen jam bands play punk songs, going silent after three minutes
and half a solo.

I've seen cubist painters sign rainbows of radiation with erasable
pen.

I've seen sneakers expand in a midsummer's orbital around the
thinly layered black whole of modern life.

I've seen towers of light explode in jehovic fury from across the pond
of godly tears.

I've seen baby filled blenders stall as they clogged with martinis and
blue label scotch.

I've seen human gods make toy guns for Arabian dummies to shoot
at like the maker's own children.

I've seen Shakespearian harmony disintegrate as the birds fled north
to the icebergs and snowstorms.

I've seen typewriters explode in antique elasticity, the writers

scratching their heads like monkeys on papyrus and sticks.

I've seen hearts ripped to shreds by vultures and teenage years.

I've seen paranoid androids win genius awards when in retrospect

the organic brilliance had faded..

I've seen water walking weirdoes with wingspans of wild and

whimsical daydreams, dreaming of deviations from the

determined destiny as they die degraded and devoid of all

perpetual predetermined peace.

I've seen cold blooded hounds chasing heroic homos from Elm Street

to river banks as the dark waters beat to the rhythm of the tell

tale heart.

I've seen seed slaying sophomores, self-righteous in their self-

evident virtuosity quote Sophocles and stupidity alike.

I've seen criminals shout out "dead man walking" before doing

cartwheels and somersaults off tenement rooftops to serve

their sentence.

I've seen donut eating diabetics drink distilled water and worship the
Übermensch and Plato.

I've seen scissor handed children cut the strings that held them up,
and cried to infinity as they died in bottomless pits.

I've seen angels climbing ladders, up and down the many steps 'til
they tire and fall to the ground.

I've seen lonely old maids raped and defiled by the very children
they nursed.

I've seen Muumuu-wearing fatsos order tabs while working their
hands to the bone for the motherland.

I've seen plastic bags suffocate in pools of acid and regurgitated spit.

I've seen glowing earlobes, glowing kneecaps, and glowing anuses.

I've seen blonde haired hipsters censor senile old horses who licked
hash browns and scrambled eggs from the melting pot of
America.

Who ran derbies instead of driving, then got old and could no longer
walk when health care ran dry and no one cared.

Who criticized the "kids these days" as their anuses ignited in

> burning feces.

Who reminisced on the future they once thought they had, and

> commented sadly on the chances lost.

* * *

I've seen self-titled movies aimed at people who were too unthinking

> to figure it out for themselves.

Who lost patience at fast food venues, eating small pox burgers just

> below their budgets.

Who drank from Uni Ball pens and poisonous rattlesnakes.

Who threw men in jail and stood by their decisions as their brothers

> coughed and wheezed in pits below their feat.

* * *

I've seen nurses in wedlock give milk to children who sucked with

teeth when they wanted more.

Who got lost in Montana and turned up ten days later with bloody

teeth and balls.

Who lusted for power bars, power vests, and power names.

Who drank water tea made of reefer leaves and honey, thinking

themselves non-conformists for smoking pot.

* * *

I've seen the last tragic heroes pass childless and broken, leaving

their legacy of greatness behind as they are lowered to their

grave to make way for the next generation of inspirational

nobodies.

Who drew assholes and underpants, speaking of writers with an

intimate irony unread by the masses.

Whose epics were published on toilet paper and cum stained

magazines.

Whose art was put on trial before aristocrats and lame stains.

Who started social revolutions by bravely admitting to being human.

Who held the flag and marched at point through starry dreams and

haze-filled lab rooms.

Who screamed "God is dead" "Humanity is dead" and "I am dead"

before a jury of their "peers."

Who, starry eyed and scabby kneed, congregated at Town Square to

watch their comrades beheaded.

Who wrote obscenities in toilet stalls again and again, each time

wasting taxpayers' money on another coat of white wash.

Who went whoring through the streets of Brooklyn, arrested three

times a night and released after a happy ending.

Who experimented with jazz and with drugs trying desperately to

reclaim the little girl lost.

Who wrote novels heralded as prophecy, later being discredited as

they first came true.

Who treated life as a game, and died of STDs after a draw.

Who smuggled pubic hair and lubricants stuffed in famous art and
diaper bags.

Who threw paper plates, paper ballots, and paper fires into
grandfather clocks in order to cause the illusion of eternity.

Who sat up cold and hungry in their third floor apartments listening
to the havoc being wreaked behind closed doors.

Who hallucinated Indian highway car crashes under the tragic sky
of a moonless mid-July night in Alabama.

Who played ping-pong and mini-golf on tenement rooftops, losing
many a ball to the heartless embrace of the Harlem River
depths.

Who lost themselves in Colorado, tending to the pool boy and tea
leaves with the care of a Post-War lover.

Who sat on beaches beneath the fat old sun, planning their journey
to meet the man in the atomic heart of the sky.

Who worshiped dada, daedra, and droppings of the greater being.

Who never surfaced from the murky waters of the Nile, but

occasionally make a guest appearance on washed up reruns

from the golden age of Hollywood.

Who acted as the eyes and the ears and the conscience, but failed.

Who ran from Rockland to Shepherdstown holding folded faces

inside canvas bag mausoleums.

Who were kept off the grass and kept out of the pools: kept in a cage

all their lives and never allowed to spread their wings and fly

to the moon.

Who leapt upwards a hundred floors to meet their doom in the

twilight of Manhattan.

Who lost their one true love to the bowels of the Atlantic.

Who picked sunflowers on the banks of dirty riverbanks, cursing the

locomotives of Moloch with their last dying breath.

Who sent flowers by phone, pressing the keys with nicotine stained

fingertips.

Who screamed in strait jackets and murdered secretaries in the

ballroom with a typewriter.

Who dropped Atom bombs fueled by cholent during first dates,

which became last ones, too.

Who dreamt of highwaymen emerging from cottages across the sea

of American loonies.

Who broke their backs lifting the city of grime and granite to the

haunted heavenly heights.

Who solved the riddle of the concrete sphinx but were ignored by

the masses whose brains were already chewed through by

worms of aluminum.

I've seen Ivory towers rust, the princesses inside growing hornets in

their hair.

I've seen brokenhearted psychics move waves of water to hide their

loves beneath the sand.

I've seen empires fall, immortals perish, and men of steel turn to ash

I've never seen an honest man.

42

I Try To Mean It When I Smile

Murderers dressed in sunday's best
commit thought-crimes inspired by divine bureaucrats
while obscure patterns radiate from an overdose on reality.
I try to mean it when I smile.

Mourners sing of hidden worlds
while haters wait for semi-inspired romantics
to write of automobiles and forgotten affairs.
I try to mean it when I smile.

Teachers sit in bombed out basements
getting stoned with future diplomats
sobbing of boredom while phones ring in faraway shacks.
I try to mean it when I smile.

Election-Day Reruns

What have you done to me?
Waking   up   early-
Running in the cold to
catch   the   bus,
These are not things I do.
Eleven-thirty-five.
I missed my wish time.

I wish I was there already-
I wish it wasn't so cold-
I wish my lungs didn't (still)
burn-
I wish gargoyles were free-
I wish vampires were friendly-
I wish I could fly & spit fire &
world.
the
save

I guess

44 In the end, a man is not defined by what he wants
But what he's willing to do to get it.

Heart Break A'int Got Nothing On Me

My Eyes Collided head on with absolutely nothing. Darkness Darker than the darkest shade of black stretched to infinity right before my eyes. Where was I? How did I get here? How the hell was I going to get back? And more importantly, did I even want to know? As my eyes adapted to the darkness, my surroundings came into focus- or rather, they didn't. I realized that my previous observations were remarkably accurate, as I was standing in the middle of what is commonly referred to as the abyss. (On a side note, I would like to mentions that anywhere in the abyss would be the middle of the abyss, as such is the nature of the abyss.) "The abyss is a funny place" I thought to myself. That was the only rational thought I had for quite some time. My next thoughts were not as much thoughts as feelings; sensations caused by the massive lack of anything substantial. I felt a pull, not that of gravity, but a yearning

Gravity has less significance when each direction is up, and each direction is down. With to go nowhere in particular. Vertigo is a funny feeling, or so I'm told. Is this vertigo? I didn't think so. There was gravity. I felt it; I felt it; I felt it pulling at me in all directions at once. I felt it pulling at me to nowhere at all.

out any discerni… , depth and distu… held no meaning what so ever. I felt warm and dizzy, yet cold and lonely. It was as if all the feelings had

Choose Your Own Adventure

The N Word

I am so Fucking Sick of hearing the N word.

Niggers,
Said the white man.
Get these goddamn Niggers out of my store.
Niggers, said the red man.
All these gang bangers running around where I live.
Niggers, said the black man.
Whatsup niggers? This shit is hot.

What the hell does Nigger Even Mean?

Theres an N–
Nothing? No one? No Hope?
Theres an I
As in me? Or impossible?
2 G's
Get Lost, Get Out.
E is for everything you know, and everyone you've lied to.
R is for rape.
Just Rape.

King Never Said Niggers.
He said the negro race, he dreamed dreams of the Negro Race.
Malcom Never Said Niggers.
Black man in the street says nigger,
White man in the street says nigger,
Spanish man in the street says nigger.

left my body, only to be rea... ...dehyde, cyanide, and Ice-N-... ...ingle somewhere between my head and everything else. The sensation was comparable to being eaten whole, digested, spit back out, blended into a soup, and then going

Seems everyone's saying it these days –

What would King say?

Nothing, cause he was shot. What would X say?

Nothing, cause he was shot.

What would I say?

Nothing. Cause I don't want to get shot.

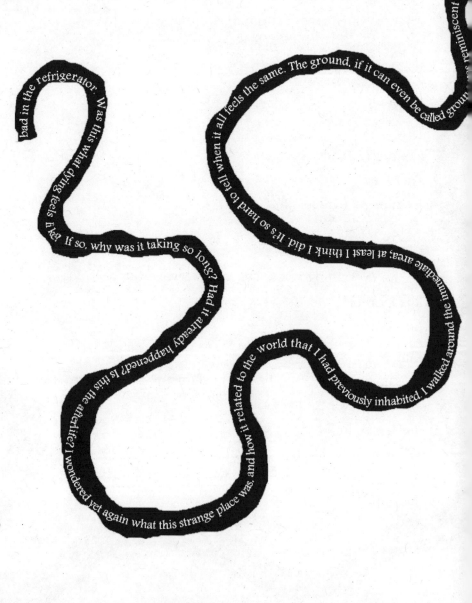

bad in the refrigerator. Was this what dying feels like? If so, why was it taking so long? Had it already happened? Is this the afterlife? I wondered yet again what this strange place was, and how it related to the world that I had previously inhabited. I walked around the immediate area, at least I think I did. It's so hard to tell when it all feels the same. The ground, if it can even be called groun...s reminiscent of cold stone floor wi...

I Once Knew A Tiger

icy glass coating. I tried to sit down, but couldn't touch the floor, as if it didn't exist. I was suspended by something I could not figure out what was supporting me. I felt as if I was having the ultimate Déjà vu, the same nothingness for eternity. I decided to walk.

It builds character,

So they say.

Why is it that everything that builds character for me,

Makes things easier for you?

Taking out the trash builds character,

Washing the dishes builds character,

Making all the beds builds character.

I've got character,

I'm funny, loud, and obnoxious.

You always tell me to quiet down.

"Shut up," you say when no one is around.

And when you're around your friends,

I'm "quite the character."

"Always moving about, that one."

I've got character.

You're old and boring,

Maybe you need to build some character.

51

Visions of My Savior

I dreamed I saw the grim reaper sitting on my windowsill
When I awoke one Monday morning feeling very ill
Good day I said how do you do can I please get you a drink
I've got chai tea perhaps earl gray some lemon zing I think
He said no thank you kind sir I cannot stop for tea
I've got a job I've got to do and with that he looked at me

I dreamed I saw jack the ripper sitting on my bedroom floor
Late one Tuesday afternoon when I opened up the door
I was taken aback a little bit but still I stood my ground
I said of all the places you could be why is it here you're found
He said to me with a voice so sweet with heavy layers of bass
I've got a thing or two to do and he looked me in the face

I dreamed I saw a heavenly angel hiding in the boiler room
Very late on Wednesday night choking on the fumes
I asked him what his business was and if he needed me
And he replied in a heavenly sigh full of certainty
My man I am hiding and with that he hung his head
For there are those among you that would wish me dead

52

or at least to give myself the illusion of walking. Where and what to, I did not know. I walked merely to walk to give myself some purpose. And so I walked and walked, and walked, and walked. without covering any distance, and without accomplishing anything other than straining myself. I got the feeling that the only reason I felt I had was because I thought I should. The only

...d my body that it ought to be hurting. Even so, on I walked, until I broke into a run. I ran like I'd never run before (which is not altogether very surprising saying as this was my first time running in the abyss). I ran, and I ran, and I ran, and I ran

...was because

NOTES

NOTES

NOTES

About the Author

Just Marino was born September 15th, 1991 – exactly sixteen years after the release of the Pink Floyd album "Wish You Were Here." Within another sixteen years, most of the text in this book was written illegibly, and typed up (somewhat legibly). This is the first completely legible collection of works by Marino, and even it, perhaps, is only partially English. In between the writing, Marino likes to pass his time making animal noises and putting them on record, as well as trying to recreate the Blues. Marino currently resides in Teaneck, New Jersey, where he spends the majority of his time pretending to be a beatnik.

ENJOYED THIS BOOK?

Log on to purchase a copy today